EGYPT IN A CUP OF TEA

Poems

By

Fabrice Guerrier

Syllble Studios

Table of Content

PART I

Lost treasures you are 3

Connections 4

Start to shine stardust 5

Destiny 6

My sweet arab tea 7

This sight too familiar 8

The fortunes will tell 9

Garden city 10

I hear this Arabian spring.. 11

PART II

Alexandria, Alexandria, Alexandria.. 13

Egypt, The Jazz you are.. 14

Peace a chance 15

Competence you must.. 16

Belief dancing belly 17

Old cairo earth that quake... 18

Perfumes of Arabian Nights 19

Storytelling.. 20

The journey train 21

PART III

Read and Meditate 23

Hourglass 24

Bring your whole self 25

Seraphim 26

The Nile of Confidence 27

Old Cairo's Roman soldiers 28

Salah Prayed..29

Egyptian Women 30

League Of Arab..31

Intentions see the future 32

This group of poems is dedicated to the 2018 Egyptian and American Fellows of the Gabr Fellowship and the Shafik Gabr Foundation.

PART I

Lost treasures you are

How dare you? How dare you! How dare you.. It ask with a blues like deja vu? How dare you seek the deepest treasures of Egypt's ancient view? When it's lost knowledge this whole whole time has lived greatly right before your eyes, as it foretold an only truth, the only destined path to take my young wild youth, to the secrets of your wonderland, to the mysteries of yourself, to the lost treasures you are, to this great work reaching your cosmic gold, those things that seep through cracks of gold, shining your joys of tears, your deepest and darkest fears, your marching armies soul, your dancing your truth to give. Stop and stop and seek not those lost treasures in Pyramids but discover the Myth of yourself! Unearth it from the sandy filled grounds below, design it with your hands, build it with all your might, repaint this great cavern of the soul, this reflection of the cosmos whole.

Connections

Connections for we are one, one with the world, already one, one with the ALL, connections to everything for the conduits of life that moves the pendulum forwards things that were in the very ancient times. Connections for we are one, ancestors and past loved ones, here, for each carries within them a piece, a soul, a momentary truth that can will shed light upon your world to see with eyes the connection the binds us ALL.

Start to shine stardust

Be original! Because everyone else is already taken. Be original for everyone else seems to have chosen a path without their thinking moving strangely like chess pieces of history. "Throw it all away" it said to me! throw away the whole squared board! move this culture inside yourself! charge the world at the door! light the truth that fire burns! let it breath on your own terms! Outside the rivers of societal flow. It said to me today "to be original!" start to shine stardust! solar bodies your cells was forged! Be original! Do things that weave great new patterns, so new ideas to who you are can be discern, don't shy away from these concerns! for it is your armor! for it is your north star!

Destiny

What you are called, the trumpet of the heavens, what you are called that things burn your will forward, it is sacred.

My sweet arab tea

My sweet sweet arab tea, Koshary hot from morning to night, I sailed your waters with a chanting decree, I sipped and sipped your blissful herbal sea which brought my tidal waves to standstill like a tree, all my dreams Hibiscus bee, all my hopes a will supreme. Your porcelain white heating vapors, I too must sing you a final plea - your dark tan waters softens my tastes, awakes flavors to the deepest of my base, from distant fields you harvest mint, that merchants lives forever Shai, wooden tables hunched my back, my sweet sweet arab tea, reflecting life's forever jazz.

This sight too familiar

We stood outside in three, surrounded by friends and kindred souls, this women like the worlds upon world approached us for her needs, her way needed help, the language lyrical, calmly asking for something, i to often had seen, the poor, the homeless asking for bread, asking for food, asking for help, I knew that look too often for it defined so much for which i was formed, forged of the poorest nations in the western world, Haiti. Yet for myself now, I saw it too on the streets of the U.S. capitol this sight was too familiar, i've seen it in Paris, in New York, in Miami, in Berlin, i've seen this plight from morning walks to work, from work to home after long days. Her eyes bent a subtle care, the hot sun, the flies, tobacco smokes and the waves of the coptic church cathedral as our backdrop, she approached.. "*Allah Ysahelek*".. the two said.. "*may the gods help you*" the two said.. I stopped later to ask upon realising what i never had i heard, a calm humility depicted through simple manners, quick and short, when the poors life here in the west are often ignored with only demeaning tones.

The fortunes will tell

When your soul is in it. When your heart is in it. When you think deeply these things always on your mind. The fortunes will tell! The fortunes will tell!

The timelines will flow! The hidden pathways will be revealed and the veil will fall in mysterious ways.

When your soul breaths truth to who you are and how you live. When your heart dances and is filled fully with the actions you take. When your mind is clear, then your moon will bring the tides to the way of the heavens. Your sun will shine the rising comos within and will sing clear the things that pull all your heart strings. The fortune will tell! The fortune will tell!

Garden city

Garden, garden city, you have captured my hearts graffiti, your classy streets and tight so neat, garden city, your building square and twisted esmeralda were all so bare, naked square tiles, blue skies of riveries, four corners and latitude, reminiscing of Paris interlude, apples red and horses chariot to hidden destinies, working destinies, working class, young living, bread, pita, cheerful breath, green and green and more green trees, staring kittens with beady eyes, rusted metal doors, garden city, your trees and trees are plentiful, your space so much they liberate.

I hear this Arabian spring

Nothing left but death, freedom and sizzling flesh. Can't you hear it? Eight years gone by yet the cries, the tears of the incinerating men who poured all over his brown body the only power he had left - his only life. Can't you hear it? This animating force, this pulsing cosmic vessel, this nucleus of symbols, this radioactive waves of unbound reality of meaning shooting arrows the hearts, the minds of this arab world for injustices that festered, stifled the art of living, that struggled the working class. Can't you feel it? Goosebump bumps rising, Can't you hear it? This men seeking freedom knowing his core will not be burned but his will to live on forever. Nursery rhymes of providence, floating impulses that none could teach, collapsing terror, rising dignity, his flesh burning to death, reborn for agonies hope to be lifted. Eight years by gone yet the sounds persisted, Can't you hear it?

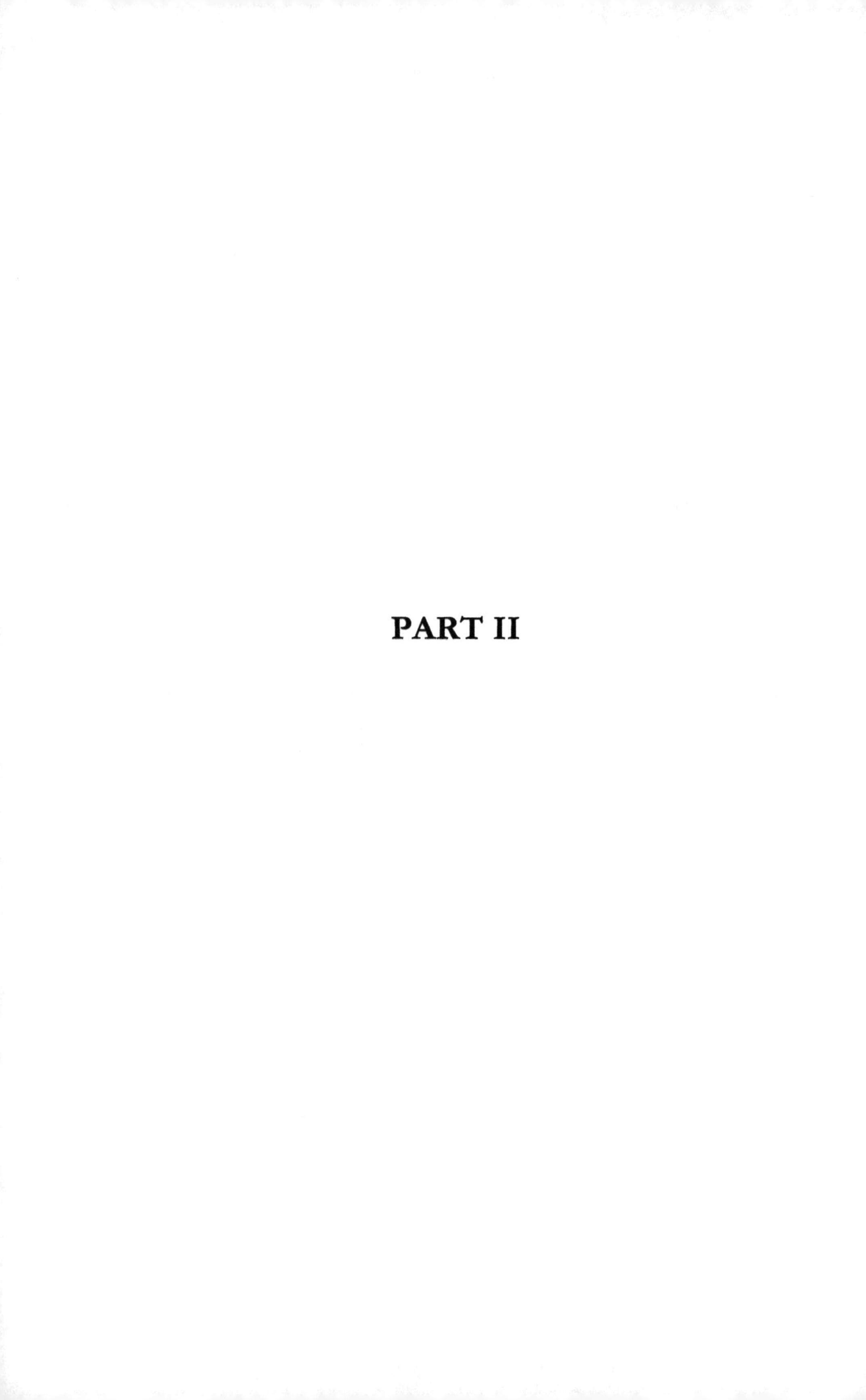

PART II

Alexandria, Alexandria, Alexandria

Purple acacias, the first time I saw them, your danced with the winds, your shaking sounds revealed, showers life shooting stairs, festive air, a familiariness beyond existed time, a familliariness that i could not explained, like a breath from the past, smells of a past that told me i was home, a theater to speak, to perform life's mystique, it was a place that became far away in the corners of my mind. The marble pillars, the gravel floor and the smells of the ocean all around, this a place i have been to, a distant soul arrived again.

Egypt, The Jazz you are

The Jazz you are, a spirit yearning for romance, a heart cracked open egg yolk, unlimited potential, crying out the ethos of an artist. A blues of body, contained like canned soup, a bomb to explode all love, music move with your walk, music with your worlds, music sings with your stare, music dances with your laughter, music souls through your people.

Peace a chance

Give peace a chance, a wound to heal festering hope, shutting pain, gushing blood

Give peace a chance, centuries in the making, of our minds and our hearts, our destiny forever interwoven

Competence you must

Competence for your tools and your god given gifts. Competence for the golden prophecy you held in your heart. Competence for your role you must play, for the journey you must take, for this becoming you will shape. Competence for the times limited, the times so small and grand to craft the future of unborn generations.

Belief dancing belly

Believe in what you do,

Your ways so sternly so

Be a warrior that challenges the world for your belief,

It's that simple

your art is freedom,

your moving body carries living beliefs, golden truths and people too, things so outwardly so, outside the minds conceiving whole.

Decide, decide and your will live on

Forever it will phenomenon

Old cairo earth that quake

The rumbled ground, shaking, people running, woman crying, priest and old man that cried that cried corners, of bodies dropping like flies, shaking earth and blood, children that hope one day but gone too soon, their brown scared, their tiny feet, their small face approached the ways of the after life, pruning the search of their lost parents

Perfumes of Arabian Nights

I will remember these smells, all the many smells that felt so new, As they swirled in the air, through my nose and to my soul, deepening joys, new heights bringing new life full of care, never dull for a second. Soulfully enticing arabian nights, I will forever remember you, your hookah endless gaze of pristine beautiful sights. Your street nights, car honking, escorts, moving bodies and all the smells that felt so new, that carried me to histories morning dew.

Storytelling

Stories are the future

they are the past

they are the way

The journey train

Life is like a train, rusted moving tracks, our hearts a compass sometimes lost. Some people stops. That capture our worlds, wondrous, mysterious and new learnings, moments that take place in the back of our minds, like the smells of arabian nights, deep friendships that anchor truth and humility, deep friendship that carves hieroglyphics of connections, unknown for now, Inside our temples, eras that last a thousands years. Packs missions and dreams, like children remembering pleasures and that never stop to live this fun. Like old men and women about to pass life is like a train remembering the playfulness of good ole times. Life is like a train, we must live full without pity, without the sadness that comes, without sadness that floods all our goodbyes.

PART III

Read and Meditate

Through reading and meditation the coptic priest he said, one may deepen the relationship to the Gods turn the gold from lead. One may grow more into love, that cosmic stream that binds all things, one may speak the language of the soul, one may walk the dance of the heart to not seek with the flesh of touch, not with the sight of the eyes, nor to speak with the words of the tongue. Through reading and meditation for you may build this house within, you may lay solid foundations with gold, expands the minds intelligence, that cosmic sense endowed to all, that common sense to always love

Hourglass

Scorching love, the sun above, grains after grains and timeless forever.

we walked into the history, who stared back at us

We walked the desert dried of our pain, drought for our deepest dreams

The Temple stood on camel backs, pyramids we were, colossal we lived, the sphinx we kissed,

The hymns we cried, we cried, for our return, the return of weavers, boulders of mountains and the grandess cities of sorrows, reject! Reject them all! Grapple your heart hand, climb the highest corridors against the shadows of god, limestone that smiled back at us

Bring your whole self

You have to merge all within you, all experience, all worlds beyond, the pasts all gone, all lives you've met, and all skills you learn on life's stage set. To be your whole self, to bring your whole selves, you have to merge all that of you, create moments that breaths gong fu. Actionless action one might call, you have to bring all the learnings, all the wisdom to deal will all the pathways unfolding around you, to do the job given to you.

Seraphim

We entered Old cairo where the energy started to rise. Angels! Angels! They were right above! as i entered this old church beloved. These angels I saw them without sight, felt them without sense, staring down their divine eyes, feathers wide, moving titanic planets merging with their ether, i saw them live through timeless love, reaching far out our every steps, blessings and cries, trumpets by their side, hidden figures moving flapping large winds into the four corners of the planet, the heavens different than us, they smiled back, they sung their movements gold as bright, guts of stars as their blood, their essence right in us. Angels! Angels! They were right above.

The Nile of Confidence

Have the confidence of the highest mountains, the himalayas, the hills of jupiter, the largest galaxies timeless to eternal might, have the confidence in knowing your talent, that flows deep as the nile, how the natural pearls given to you by divine providence can be polished, so let it be, polish them, take them for the precious things they are. For they can shine thousands of ways that live true to who you are. Be true, be honest and educate yourself with the riches of all things (paintings, music, politics, social, nature, people, history, sciences, movies, myths..) educate yourself for it will be the ship that will sail and shape the greatest art of it all, the art of living

Old Cairo's Roman soldiers

The coptic ways, i saw them, the romans brown silvery backs, horns on shoulders pads, metal sticks and handless of defence that marched and marched with the deepest of pride to defend for themselves all the fears that had crept, that could crept, i saw them, i saw them the silvery sounds bit by bit, the shackles untied.

Salah Prayed

I bowed down to the floor that formed a dot of truth, it layed that time and showed on my forehead sooth. I bowed down to the divine, to pray my love to you, to chant my chants, my ways renewed. I bent my knees to the almighty to give blessings for all that i shall build with you. I bowed down down to the divine, for the ways of life, for the ways that you could heal, to my closenessness with you I raised to God, I praised this world that i was born, with no regrets that I can breath and can dance once more.

Egyptian Women

In your eyes i saw the whole universe, the stars & perfections compared to distant nebulas. In your smiles i felt history of ancient arab worlds, hidden stories and thriving isis, magic pulsing your endless charms. In your skin, I saw the mother of the world, civilizations tapestry and births of endless forthcoming worlds.

League Of Arab

I saw history weave itself in the room, an idea fused to life, fused to now, the passing winds, the wooden frames and dancing leaves, weaved themselves a hidden way to its birth they too witness the Arab League. We sat with its secretary general living the hopes of the east and the west of their past dreams. The light corners extended a maturity that sat too calmy with the space so grand. Our tears, sweet and brown, our quest yet to be discovered born from a world war, the plight of mankind, the differential quest for power, the blind eyes of lady justice, the karma of our wishes.

Intentions see the future

Set your intentions, turn the tides of history to your god head, pour the precious wines to the clear glass of our life, set your intentions now and the universe will move out of the way and bring forth those deepest of desires! Greatly take the net that captures all of you and anchor your compass, the souls spirit, a creative force that lives everywhere, in everything, in the now and every of your futures.

www.ingramcontent.com/pod-product-compliance
Lightning Source LLC
Chambersburg PA
CBHW032134050726
47590CB00008B/3090